THE SECRET GRIMOIRE
OF TURIEL

THE SECRET GRIMOIRE
OF TURIEL

A SYSTEM OF CEREMONIAL MAGIC
THE GREAT ARCANUM
(The Rites of Ceremonial Magick).

PART THE FIRST

OBSERVATIONS and method of Invoking related with great pains and diligent research.

Retire thyself Seven Days free from all company and fast and pray from sunset to sunrise. Rise every morning at Seven of the clock, and the three days previous to the Work fast upon bread and water and humble thyself before Almighty God.

Watch and pray all night before the Work.

And on the day before draw the lines of the Circle in a fair place. and let the diameter of the Circle be 9 feet. Wash thyself the same day quite clean. Make the pentacles forthwith and provide the other things necessary, with Incensing. Then being clothed in pure Vestments and having covered the Altar and lighted the candles begin about half an hour before sunrise on the Day assigned for the Work and say with great Devotion as follows

First Morning Prayer

Almighty and Most Merciful Father I beseech Thee that Thou wilt vouchsafe favorably to hear me at this time whilst I make my humble prayer and Supplication unto Thee. I confess unto Thee O Lord Thou hast justly punished me for my manifold sins and offences but Thou hast promised at what time so ever a sinner doth repent of his sins and wickedness Thou wilt pardon and forgive him and turn away the remembrance of them from before Thy face.

Purge me therefore O Lord and wash me from all my offences in the Blood of Jesus Christ that, being pure and clothed in the Vestments of Sanctity, I may bring this Work to perfection, through Jesus our Lord who liveth and reigneth with Thee in the Unity of the Holy Ghost. Amen.

Sprinkle thyself with Holy Water and say

Asperges me Domine hysope, et mundabor. Lavabis me et super nivem dealbabor.

Hail O Mighty God, for in Thy power alone abideth the Key to all exorcising of Principalities, Powers, Thrones, Angels and Spirits. Amen.

Then bless your Girdle, saying

O God Who by the breath of Thy nostrils framed Heaven and Earth and wonderfully disposed all things therein in six days, grant that this now brought to perfection by Thine unworthy servant may be by Thee blessed and receive Divine virtue, power and Influence from Thee that every thing therein contained may fully operate according to the hope and confidence of me Thine time worthy servant through Jesus Christ our Lord and Saviour. Amen.

The Blessing of the Light

I bless thee in the Name of the Father. O Holy, Holy Lord, God, Heaven and Earth are fuil of Thy Glory before Whose face there is a bright shining light forever; bless now, O Lord, I beseech Thee, these creatures of light which Thou hast given for the Kindly use of man that they, by Thee being sanctified, may not be put out or extinguished by the power, malice, or filthy darkness of the devil, but may shine forth brightly and lend their assistance to this my Work, through Jesus Christ our Lord. Amen.

Then say, 'Asperges me, etc."

Consecration of the Sword

O Great God Who art the God of strength and fortitude and greatly to be feared, bless O Lord, this Instrument that it may be a terror unto the Enemy, and therewith I may fight with and overcome all phantasms and oppositions of the Enemy, through the influence and help of Thy most Holy Mighty Name, On, St. Agla, and in the Cross of Jesus Christ our only Lord. Amen.

Be thou blessed and consecrated in the Name of the Father, Son, and Holy Ghost. Asperges me, etc.

Benediction of the Lamens
(Symbois. Circles)

O God Thou God of my Salvation I call upon Thee by the mysteries of Thy most holy Name, On, St. Agla, I worship and beseech Thee by Thy Names El, Elohim, Elohe, Zebaoth, and by Thy Mighty Name Tetragrammaton, Saday, that Thou wilt be seen in the power and force of these Thy most holy names so written filling them with divine virtue and Influence through Jesus Christ our Lord.

Benediction of the Pentacles

Eternal God which, by Thy Holy Wisdom, hast caused great power and virtue to lie hidden in the characters and Holy Writings of Thy Spirits and Angels, and hast given unto man that with them, faithfully used, power thereby to work many things; bless these, O Lord, framed and written by the hand of me Thine unworthy servant that being filled with divine virtue and Influence by Thy Commands, O Most Holy God, they may shew forth their virtue and power to Thy praise and Glory through Jesus Christ our Lord. Amen.

I bless and consecrate you in the Name of the Father, the Son, and the Holy Ghost, the God of Abraham, Isaac, and Jacob. Asperges me, etc. Amen.

Benediction of the Garment

O Holy, blessed and Eternal Lord God Who art the God of purity and delightest that our souls should appear before Thee in clean and pure and undefiled Vestments being cleansed, blessed, and consecrated by Thee, I may put them on, being therewith clothed I may be whiter than snow both in soul and body in Thy presence this day, in and through the ment, death, and passion of our onty Lord and Saviour Jesus Christ, Who liveth and reigneth with Thee in the Unity of the Holy Spirit, ever one God, world without end. The God of Abraham, Isaac and Jacob bless thee, purge thee, and make thee pure, and be thou clean in the Name of the Father, Son and Holy Ghost. Amen.

In this Thy Holy Sign O God, I fear no evil. By Thy Holy Power, and by this Thy Holy Sign all evil doth flee.

By Thy Holy Name and Thy Power which Secret was revealed to Moses, through the Holy Names written in this Book, depart far from me all ye workers of iniquity.

Bless, O Lord, I beseech Thee, this place and drive away all evil and wickedness far from it. Sanctify and make it become meet and convenient for Thy Servant to finish and bring to pass therein his desires, through Jesus Christ our Lord, Amen.

Be thou blessed and purified in the Name of the Father, Son, ami Holy Ghost. Amen.

Benediction of the Perfumes

The God of Abraham, the God of Isaac, the God of Jacob, bless here the creatures of these kinds that they may give forth the power of their odours so that neither the Enemy nor any false Imaginaions may be able to enter into them, through our Lord Jesus Christ, to whom be honour and Glory now, henceforth, and for ever. Amen.

Sprinkle them with Holy Water, saying, "Asperges me, Domine, etc."

Exorcism of Fire

I exorcise thee, O thou creature of Fire, by Him by Whom all things are made, that forthwith thou wilt cast away every phantasm from thee that it shall not be able to do any hurt in any thing. Bless, O Lord, this creature of Fire and sanctify it, that it may be biessed to set forth the praise of Thy Holy Name that no hurt may be able to come unto me, through the virtue and defence of our Lord Jesus Christ. Amen.

HAZEL TWIG WAND (FORKED

HAZEL WAND

SWORD

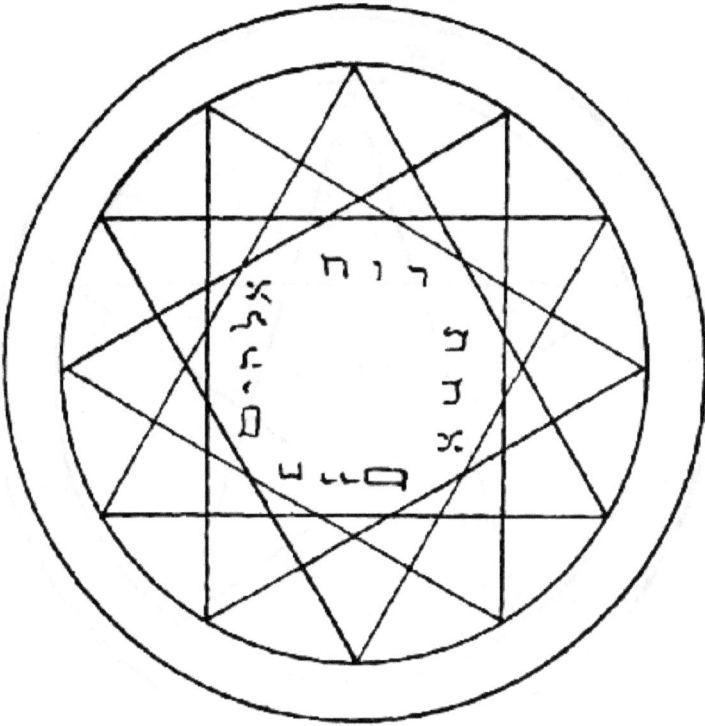

Invocation for Sunday
(SOL)

Come, Heavenly Spirits who have the effulgent rays of the Sun, Luminous Spirits who are ready to obey the power of the great Tetragrammaton, come and assist me in the operation that I am making under the auspices of the Grand Light of Day whicb the Eternal Creator hath formed for the use of universal nature. I invoke you for these purposes. Be favourable and auspicious to what I shali ask in the Name of Amioram, Adonai, Sabaoth.

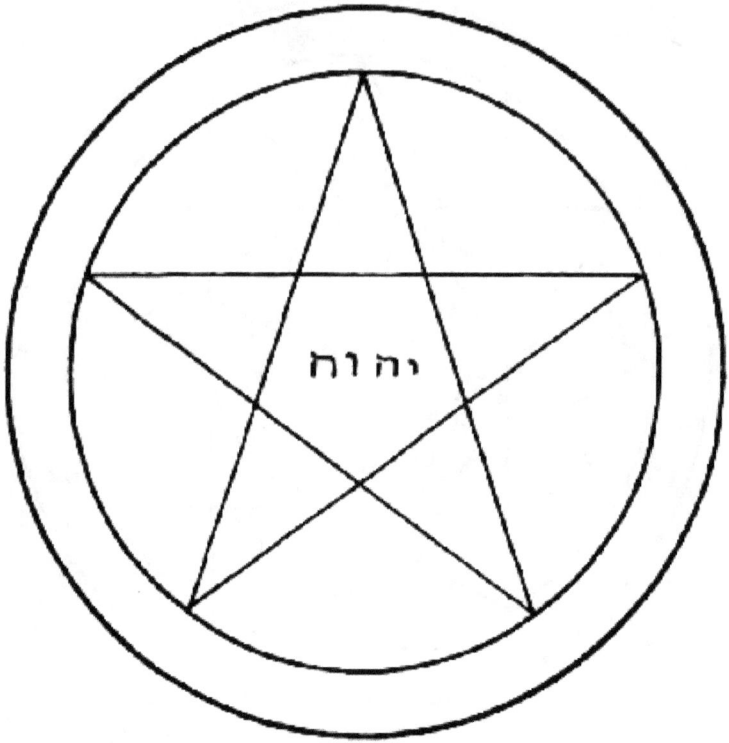

Invocation for Monday
(MOON)

Haste ye Sublime and Intelligent Genil who are obedient to the Sovereigu Arcana, come and assist me in the operation that I undertake under the auspices of the Grand Lumiriary of the Night. I invoke you to this end and implore you to be favourable and hear my entreaties in the Name of Him Who commands the spirits of the Four Quarters of the Universal Mansions: Inhabit, Bileth, Mizabu, Abinzaba.

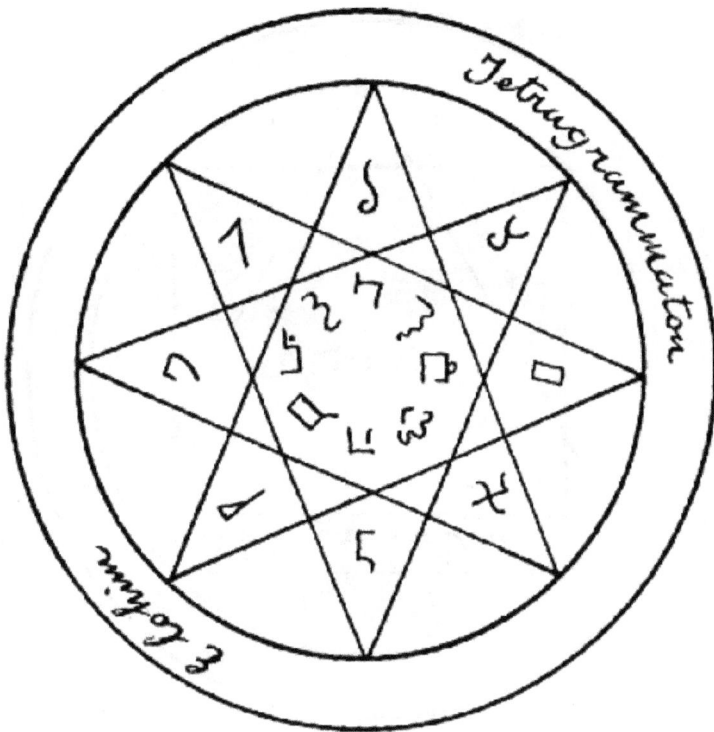

Invocation for Tuesday
(MARS)

Come Children of the Red Genii who have executed the order of the Sovereign Master of the Universe upon the armies of the rash Sennacherib, come and assist me in the operation that I undertake under the auspices of the third brilliant luminary of the firmament; be favourable to my entreaties in the Name of Adonay Sabaoth.

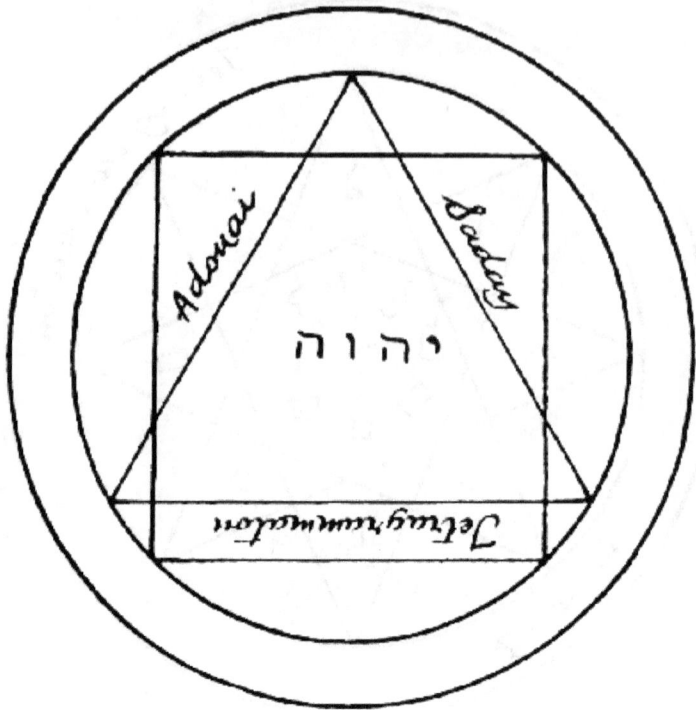

Invocation of Wednesday
(MERCURY)

Run to me with speed, come to me ye Spirits of Mercury who preside over the operation of this day, hear favourably the present invocation that I make to you under the Divine Names of Venoel, Uranel, be kind and ready to second my undertakings. Render them efficacious.

Invocation for Thursday
(JUPITER)

Come speedily ye Olepid Spirits who preside over the operation of this day.

Come, Incomprehensible Zebarel and all your legions, haste to my assistance and be propitious to my undertakings, be kind and refuse me not your powerful aid and assistance.

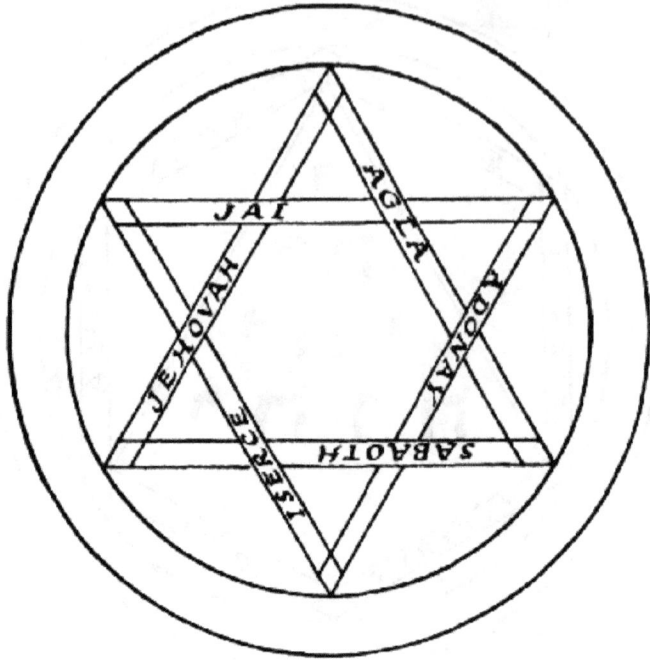

Invocation for Friday
(VENUS)

Come on the wings of the wind, ye happy Genii who preside over the workings of the heart. Come in the Name of the Great Tetragrammaton; hear favourably the Invocation that I make this day, destined to the wonder of love. Be ready to lend me your assistance to succeed in what I have undertaken under the hope that you will be favourable to me.

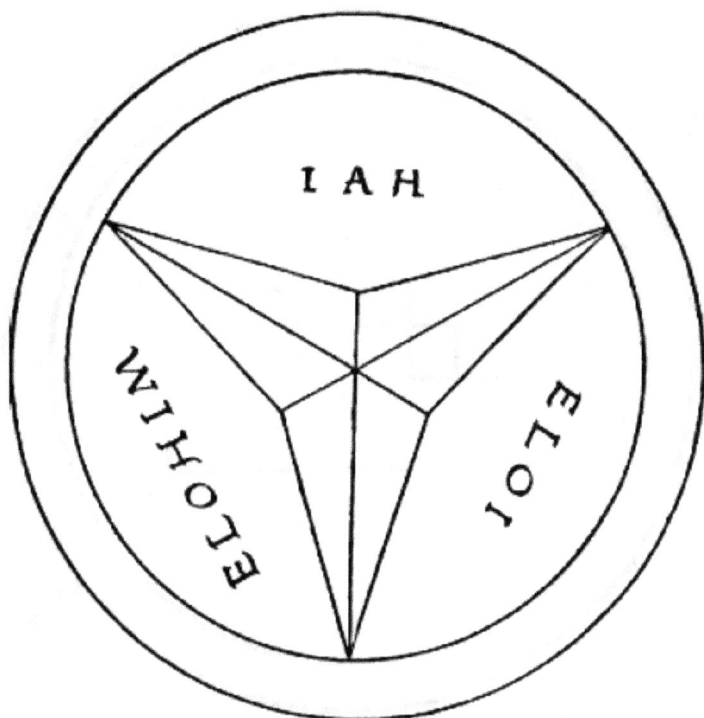

Invocation for Saturday
(SATURN)

Come out of your gloomy solitude ye Saturnine spirits, come with your cohort, come with diligence to the place where I am going to begin my operation under your auspices; be attentive to my labours and contribute your assistance that it may rebound to the honour and glory of the Highest.

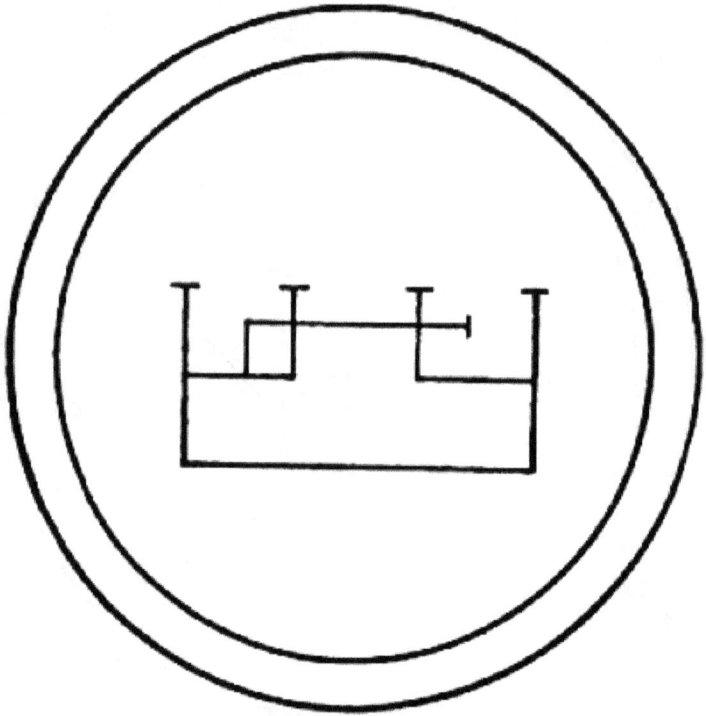

CHARACTER OF ARATRON LORD OF SATURN

Perfumes

Saifron, with the wood of Atoes, the Elder and the Pine. Add to it a grain of Musk, and consecrate the whole, pulverized and mixed together in a paste.

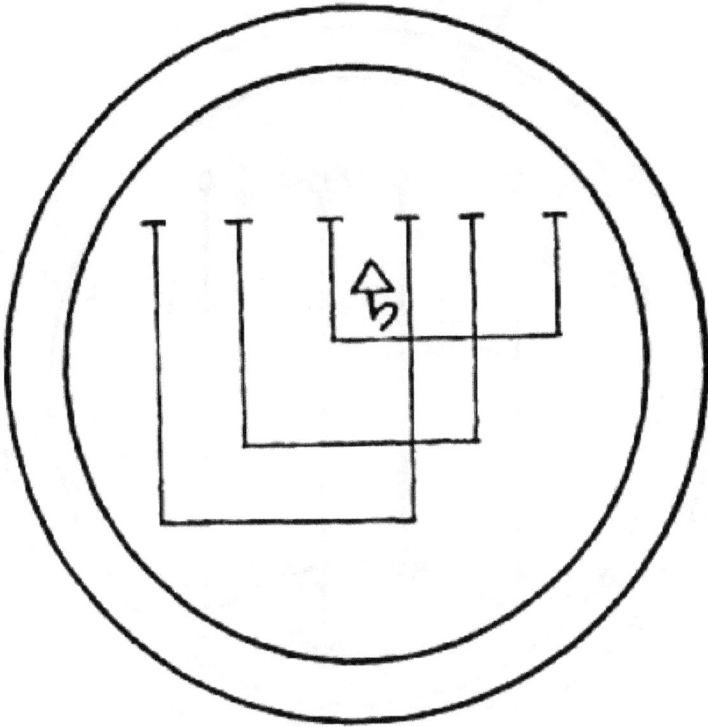

CHARACTER OF PRALEG LORD OF MARS

Perfumes

The head of a frog, the Bovine Blood, a grain of White Poppy, Fiowers of Camomile, and Camphor, pulverized into a paste by the mixing of the blood of a Virgin Kid.

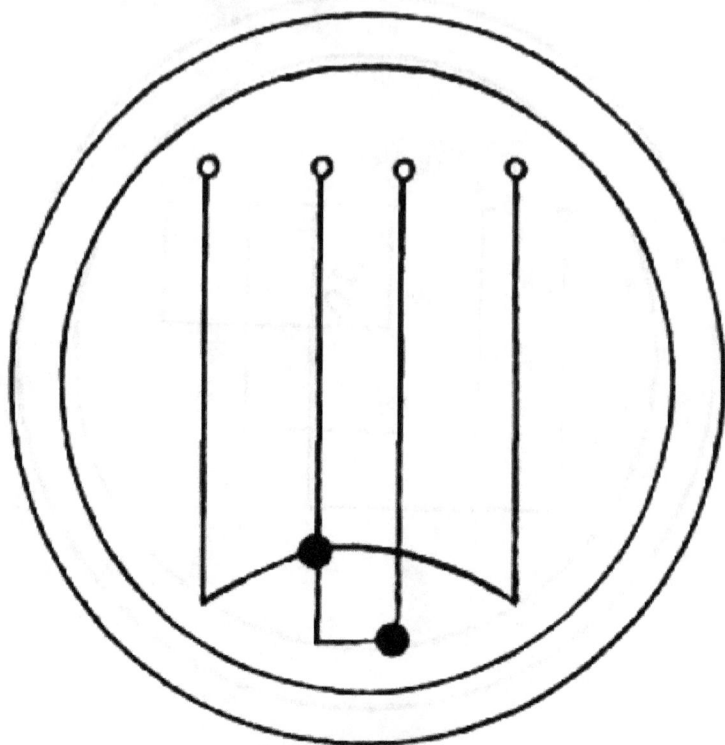

CHARACTER of PHUL LORD OF THE Moon

Perfumes

Leaves of the Mandrake, Sal Ammonia, Roots of Gentian, Valerian herbs finely cut, a little Sulphur, made into a paste with the blood of a black Cat.

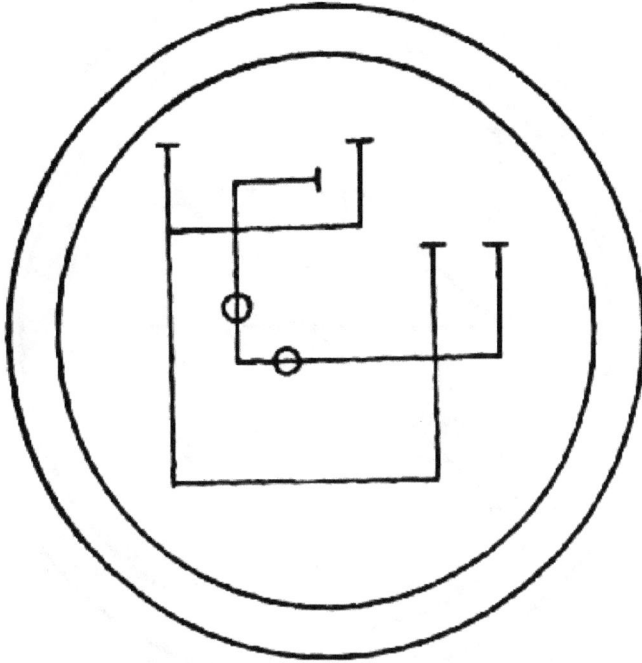

CHARACTER OF JETHOR LORD OF JUPITER

Perfumes

Sandalwood of the East, leaves of Agrimony, Choves, powder of Henbane. Beat all into a powder. Make thereof a paste with Foxes' blood and the brains of a Magpie.

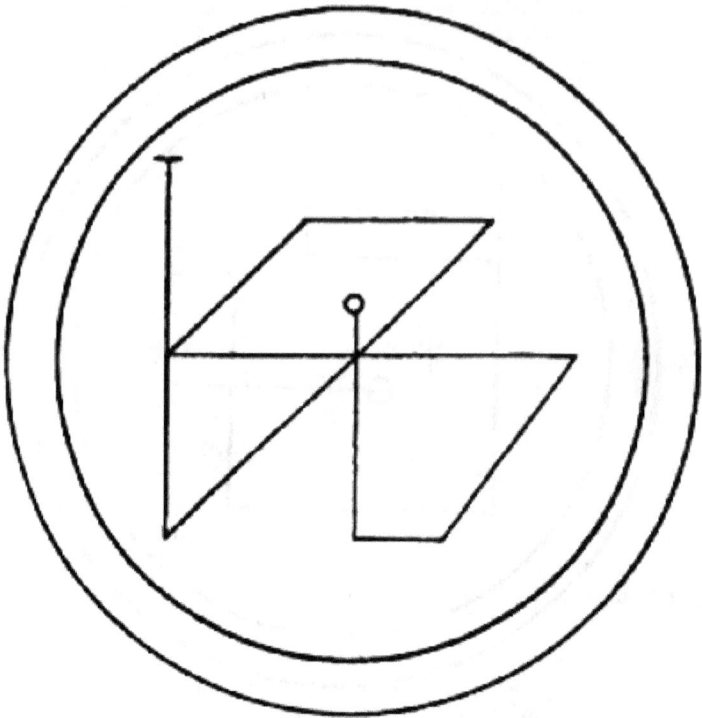

CHARACTER OF OPHIEL LORD OF MERCURY

Perfumes

The seed of an Ash Tree, the wood of the Aloe, leaves of the Scullcap Herb, Mandrake roots, and the end of a Quili, made into small balls (pihis).

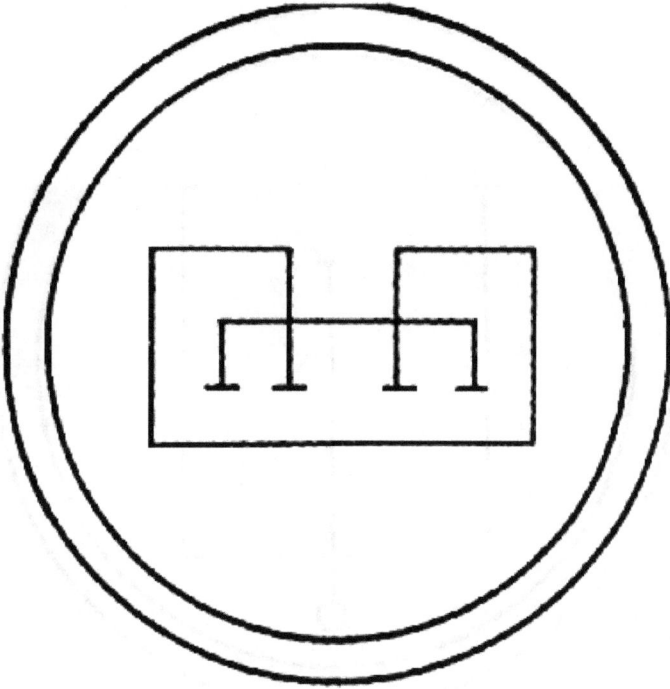

CHARACTER OF HAGITH LORD OF VENUS

Perfumes

Musk, Juniper berries, wood of Áloes, dried Red Roses, dried leaves of Elder, pulvenzed, and made into a paste with the blood of a Pigeon.

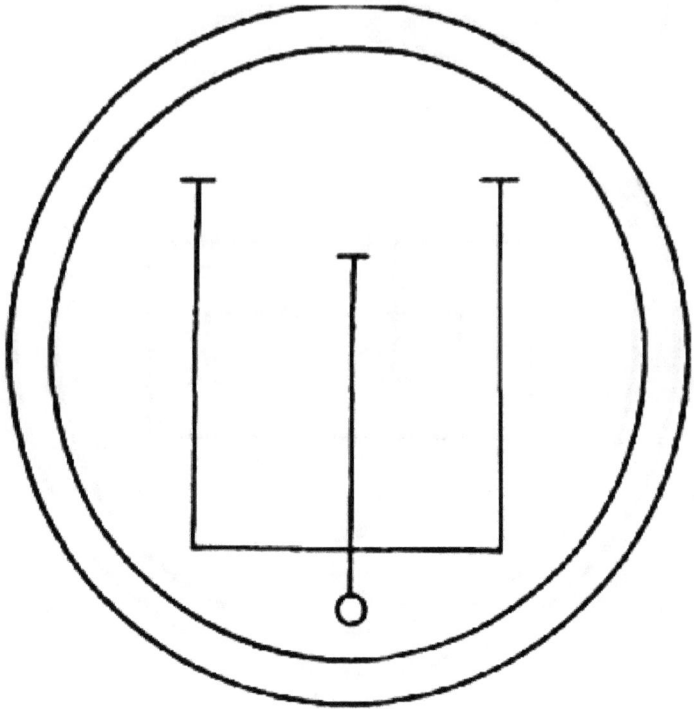

CHARACTER OF OCH LORD OF THE SUN

Perfumes

Grains of Bhack Pepper, grains of Hogsbane, powder of Sulphur, made into a paste with the blood of a Bat, and the brains of a black Cat.

PART THE SECOND

CONTAINING INVOCATIONS, CONJURATIONS, ARO EXORCISMS OF TREE BAND OF SPIRITS

FORM OF CONJURING AND EXORCISING SPIRITS TO

Oration lo be said when putting on the Vestures

Amacor, Amacor, Amides, Theodomai, Aintor, by the merits of Thy Angels, O Lord, I with I put on the garments of Righteousness, that this which I desire I may bring to perfection through the most holy Adonay, Whose kingdom endureth for ever and ever. Amen.

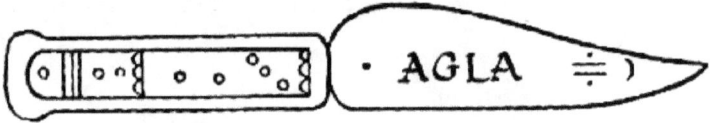

This on the other side

The Lamen

Prayer

Holy, Holy Lord God, from Whom all holy desires do proceed, I beg Thou wilt be merciful unto me at this time, granting I may become a True Magician and contemplate of Thy wondrous works at alt times, in the Name of the Father and of the Son. Therefore in al! my doings and at all times I will call upon Thy Most Holy Name, O Lord, for Thy help and assistance.

I beseech Thee, O Lord, that Thou wilt purge me and wash me iii the blood of our Saviour, from al! my sins and frailties, and that Thou wilt henceforward vouchsafe to keep and defend me from pride, lusts, cursing, blasphemy, unfaithfulness, and al! other deadly sins and enormous offences, profaneness and spiritual wickedness ; but that I may lead a godhy, saber, faithful, constant and pure life, walking uprightly in Thy sight, through the merits of Jesus Christ, Thy Son, our Lord and Saviour.

Omnipotent and Eternal Lord God Who sittest in Heaven and dost from thence behoid alt the dwehlers upon earth, most mercifully I beseech Thee to hear and answer the petition of Thine unworthy servant, which I shali make unto Thee at this time, through Jesus Christ our Lord, Who hiveth and reigneth with Thee in the unity of Thy Holy Spirit, ever One God, world without end.

Sead down, O Lord, the Spirit of Thy Grace upon me. O God, put fear far from me, and give me an abundance in Thy faith, whereby all things are made possible unto man; put every wicked phantom far from my mind, and grant me true zeal, fervor, and intentive spirit of zeal, and prayer, that I may offer up a well-pleasing sacrifice unto Thee. Let me use Thy ministering spirits and Angels,O Lord, as thereby I may attain true wisdom and knowledge.

Our Father, etc.

Credo, etc.

Ave Maria, etc.

Glory be to the Father, Son, and Holy Ghost; as it was in the beginning, is now, and ever shalll be, world without end. Amen.

Holy, Holy, Holy, Lord God of Sabaoth, which will come to judge the quick and the dead; Thou art Alpha and Omega, the first and the last, King of Kings, and Lord of Lords, Ioth, Abiel, Anathiel, Aniasim, Alganabro, El, Sedomel, Gayes,

Hehi, Messias, Tolosm, Elias, Eschiros, Athanatos; by these Thy Holy Names, and al! others, I do call upon Thee and beseech Thee, O Lord, by Thy Nativity and baptism, by Thy Cross and Passion, by Thine ascension, and by the coming of Thy Holy Ghost, by the bitterness of Thy Soul when it departed from Thy body; by Thine Angels, Archangels, prophets, patriarchs, and by all Thy Saints, and by alt the Sacraments which are made in Thine honour, I do worship and beseech Thee, I bless and desire Thee, to accept these prayers and conjurations. I implore Thee, O Holy Adonay, Amay, Horta, Vegadoro, Ysion, Ysesy, and by all Thy Holy Names, and by al! Thine Angels, Archangels, and Powers, Dominations, and Virtues, and by Thy Name with which King Solomon did bind up the devils and shut them up, Ethrack, Evanher, Agla, Goth, Joth, Othie, Venock, Nabrat, and by all Thy Holy Names which are written in this book, and by the virtue of them all, that Thou enable me to congregate all Thy spirits, that they may give me true answers to all my demands.

O Great and Eternal Virtue of the Highest, which Thou disposest their being come to judgment, Viachem, Stimilomaton, Esphares, Tetragrammaton, Oboram, Cryon, Elijtion, Onela, Brassim, Aoym, Messias, Soter, Emanuel, Sabaoth, Adonay, I worship Thee. I implore Thee with all the strength of my mind that by Thee my present prayers, consecrations, and conjurations may be hallowed. In the Name of the most merciful God of Heaven and of Earth, of the Seas and of the Infernais, by Thine Omnipotent help may I perform this Work.

Helie, Helion, Esseju, Deus Eternis, Eloy, Clemens Deus, Sanctus Sabaoth, Deus Exercillum, Adonay, Deus Mirabilis, Jao, Verax, Ampheneton, Saday, Dominator, On, Fortissimus Deus, invest with Thy blessed help this Work begun of Thee, that it may be consummated by Thy mighty power. Amen.

Amoruli, Tametia, Latisten, Rabur, Tanetia, Latisten, Escha, Aloelin, Alpha et Omega, Leytse, Oraston, Adonay. Amen.

Names and Offices of the Spirits. Messengers. and Intelligences of the Seven Planets

Spirits of the Sun

Gabriel.
Vianathraba.
Corat.

Messengers of the Sun.

Burchat.
Suceratos.
Capabile.

Intelligences of the Sun.

HaludieL
Machasiel.
Chassiel.

Spirits of the Moon.

Gabriel.
Gabraei.
Madios.

Messengers of the Moon.

Anael.
Pabael.
Ustael.

Intelligences of the Moon.

Uriel.
Naromiel.
Abuori.

Spirits of Saturn.

Samael.
Bachiel.
Astel.

Messengers of Saturn.

Sachieh.
Zoniel.
Hubaril.

Intelligences of Saturn.

Mael.
Orael.
Valnum.

Spirits of Jupiter.

Setchiel.
Chedusitanieh.
Corael

Messengers of Jupiter.

Tunel. (See Secret Grimoire of Turiel).
Conieh.
Babiel.

Intelligences of Jupiter.
Kadiel.
Maltiel.
Huphatrieb.
Estael.

Spirits of Venus.

Thamael.
Tenariel.
Arragon.

Messengers of Venus.

Coiznas.
Peajel
Penael.

Intelligences of Venus.

Penat.
Thiel.
Rael
Teriapel.

Spirits of Mercury.

Mathlai.
Tarmiel.
Baraborat.

Messengers of Mercury.

Raphael.
Ramel.
Doremiel.

Intelligences of Mercury.

Aiediat.
Modiat.
Sugmonos.
Sallales.

Presiding Spirits of Jupiter.

Sachiel.
Castiel.
Asasiel.

Presiding Spirits of Venus.

Anael.
Rachiel.
Sachiel.

Presiding Spirits of Mars.

Samael.
Satael.
Amabiel.

Presiding Spirits of Mercury.

Raphael.
Uriel.
Seraphiel.

Angeli Glorioso supradicti estote coadjutores et auxiliatores
in omnibus negotijs et interrogationibus in omnibus celensq
causis per Eum qui venturus est judiciase vivos et mortuos.

Omnipotent and Eternal God Who hast ordained the whole
creation for Thy praise and glory and for the salvation of
man, I earnestly beseech Thee that Thou wouldst send one
of Thy spirits of the Orden of Jupiter, one of the messengers
of Sachiel whom Thou hast appointed presiding spirit of
Thy firmament at this time, most faithfully, willingly to show
unto me those things which I shall demand or require of
him, and truly execute my desires. Nevertheless, O most
Holy God, Thy will and not mine be done, through Jesus
Christ our Lord. Amen.

Invocation

I call upon thee, Sachiel, Castiel, and Asasiel, in the Name
of the Father, and of the Son, and of the Holy Ghost,
Blessed Trinity, Inseparable Unity, I invoke and entreat thee,
Sachiel, Castiel, and Asasiel, in this hour to attend to the
words and conjurations which I shall use by the Holy Names
of God, El, Elohim, Elohe, Eeoba, Sabaoth, Elion, Eschiros,
Adonay, Jay, Tetragrammaton, Saday; I conjure and excite
you by the Holy Names of God, Hagios, Otheos, Ischyros,
Athanatos, Paracletos, Agla, On, Alpha and Omega, Ausias,

Tolimi, Elias, Irnos, Aniay, Horta, Vegadora, Antir, Sibranat, Amatha, Baldachia, Anuoram, Anexpheton, Via, Vita, Manus, Fons, Origo, Filius

יהוה

and by all the other Holy, Glorious, Great, and Unspeakable, Mysterious, Mighty, Powerful, and Incomprehensible Names of God, that you attend unto the words which I shall utter, and send unto me Tarje!, Coniel, on Babiel, messengers of your sphere, to tell unto me such things as I shall demand of him, in the Name of the Father, Son, and Holy Ghost.

I entreat thee, Setchiel, Chedustaniel, and Corael, by the whole host of Heaven, Seraphims, Cherubims, Thrones, Dominations, Virtues, Powers, Principalities, Archangels and Angels, by the great and giorious Spirits Orphaniel, Tetra, Pagiel, Salmia, Pastor, Salun, Azimor, and by your Star which is Jupiter, and by all the constellations of Heaven, and by whatsoever you obey, and by your Character which you have given and proposed and confirmed, that you attend unto me according to the prayers and petitions which I have made unto Almighty God, and that you forthwith send unto me one of your messengers who may willingly and truly and faithfully fulfill all my desires, wishes and commands, and that you command him to appear unto me in form of a beautiful angel clothed in white vestures, gently, courteously, kindly, and affably entering into communication with me, and that he neither bring terror nor fear unto me, or obstinately deny my requests, neither permitting any evil spirits to appear or approach in any way to hurt, terrify, or affright me, nor deceiving me in any wise; through the virtue of our Lord and Saviour Jesus Christ, in Whose Name I attend, waiting for and expecting your appearance. Fiat, Fiat, Fiat. Amen.

Interrogations

"Comest thou in peace, in the Name of the Father, and of the Son, and of the Holy Ghost "

"Yes".

"Thou art welcome, noble Spirit. What is thy name?"

"Turiel ".

"I have called thee here, Turiel, in the Name of Jesus of Nazareth, at Whose Name every knee doth bow, both of things in Heaven, Earth, and Heil, and every tongue shall confess there is no Name like unto the Name of Jesus, Who hath given power unto man to bind and to loose all things in His Name, yea, even unto them that trust in His salvation. Art thou the messeager of Setchiel"

"yes"

"Wilt thou confirm thyself unto me at this time, and from henceforward reveal all things unto me that I shall desire to know and teach me how to increase my wisdom and knowledge, and show unto me the secrets of the Magick Art, and of the liberal sciences, that I may set forth the praise and glory of Almighty God"

"Yes".

"Then, I pray thee, give and confirm thy Character unto me, whereby I may call thee at al! times, and also swear unto me this Oath, and I will righteously keep my vow and covenant unto Almighty God, and will courteously receive thee at all times when thou dost appear to me

"Forasmuch as thou camest in peace and quietness and hast answered me and unto my petitions, I give humble and hearty thanks unto Almighty God, in whose Name I called thee and thou camest. And now thou mayest depart in peace unto thy Orders, and return unto me again at what time soever I shall call thee by Licence to Depart

"thine own Oath, or by thy name, or by thine Order, or by thine Office which is granted from the Creator. And the Grace of God be with thee and me and upon the whoie Israel of God. Amen.

"Glory be to the Father, and to the Son, and to the Holy Ghost, as it was in the beginning, is now, and ever shall be, world without end. Fiat. Fiat. Fiat. Amen ".

Form of a Bond of Spirits given by Turiel, Messenger of the Spirits of Jupiter:

Gloria Deo in Excelsis.

יהוה

I, Turiel, Messenger of the Spirits of Jupiter, appointed thereunto by the Creator of all things visible and invisible, do swear and promise, and plighting faith and troth unto thee in the presence, by, and before the Great Lord of Heaven and the whole company of Heaven, by all the Holy Names of God, do swear and bind myself unto thee, by all the contents of God's Sacred Writ, by the Incarnation, death and passion, resurrection, and glorious Ascension of Jesus Christ, by all the Holy Sacraments, by the Mercy of God, by the Glory and Eyes of Heaven, by the forgiveness of sin, and hope of eternal salvation, by the Great

Day of Doom, by all the Angels and Archangels, Seraphim, Cherubim, Dominations, Thrones, Principalities, Powers, and Virtues, Patriarchs, Prophets, Saints, Martyrs, Innocents, and all others of the blessed and glorious Company of Heaven, and by all the sacred powers and virtues above rehearsed, and by whatever is holy and binding, thus do I swear now, and promise unto thee that I will hasten unto thee, and appear clearly unto thee at all times and places, and in all hours, days, and minutes, from this time forward until thy life's end, whensoever thou shalt call me by my name, or by my Office, and will come unto thee in what form thou shalt desire, whether it be visibly or invisibly; I will answer all thy desires. And in testimony whereof, and before all the Powers of Heaven, I have hereunto set, subscribed, and confirmed my Character unto thee.

So help me God. Fiat. Amen.

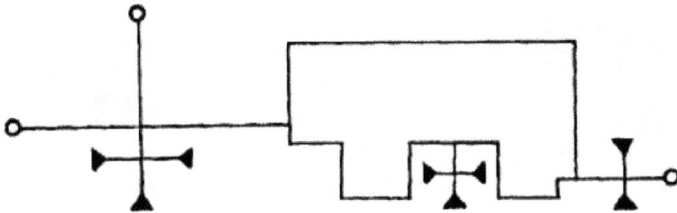

The Character of Turiel.

FINIS

www.ingramcontent.com/pod-product-compliance
Lightning Source LLC
Chambersburg PA
CBHW060526110426
42741CB00042B/2792